Our Wedding

SCRAPBOOK

And so it begins...

Planning a wedding is an exciting time, filled with many surprises and special moments. I have designed this book to help you create a visual keepsake not only of your wedding day itself, but also of everything from your first date to your honeymoon and even your wedding anniversaries. I hope you and your family will use this book to relive all your wonderful memories.

Make this book your own. Just like your wedding, there are no strict rules. Do not worry about filling out every page or following every suggestion. Paste your own ideas and memories over pages that do not apply. Personalize this book—your book—with your own notes and touches.

Here are a few tips to help you get started:

- Flip through the book now to get an idea of the types of memorabilia you may want to keep, even if you do not plan to begin making your scrapbook right away.
- Keep a small camera handy in your bag so that you can capture important and amusing moments as you go along.
- At your wedding, give your photographer a shot list and schedule, so you are sure to capture special moments, details, and people on film.
- Save fabric swatches, notes, and other special mementos, even if it means asking friends and relatives to write down their toasts.
- If you cannot fit everything you want to include on the pages that follow, use a computer or a color copier to shrink images, copies of a toast, your seating chart, or your marriage license. You can also make collages using color copies of contact sheets.
- Paste envelopes on the pages to hold fabric swatches or other items. Use clips (either decorative or simple paper clips) to attach mementos or lists with multiple pages (e.g., your bridal registry).
- To help preserve the contents of your scrapbook, consider archival/photo-safe glue or tape, archival mist, or photo corners.

In short, have fun with it! Whenever my husband Andy and I look at our own wedding scrapbook, everything comes back to us as if it happened yesterday. Best of all, we can't wait to show it to our children.

Enjoy your wedding—and your scrapbook!

Darcy Miller

clip if you choose

Our Wedding

BRIDE

TO

GROOM

WEDDING DATE

Us:

How we met

Our first date

When we knew this was THE ONE

The Courtship

Our favorite things:
places, songs, things we laughed about, movies, nicknames for each other, trips...

place photos or memorabilia from when you were dating

The Proposal

Where?

When?

How?

The best part was...

place photos or special mementos (matchbooks from the restaurant, page from your calendar, ticket stub from the trip, etc.)

The Day We Got Engaged

Whom we told, what they said, how we celebrated

Our Families

carve your initials in the heart

When we met each other's families

When our families first met each other

How we think it went

paste photos of your friends and families here (perhaps from your parents' weddings)

Our Engagement Celebration

Where was it held? Who hosted? Who was there?

Memorable toasts, advice, and wishes

place invitation, menu, mementos, photos

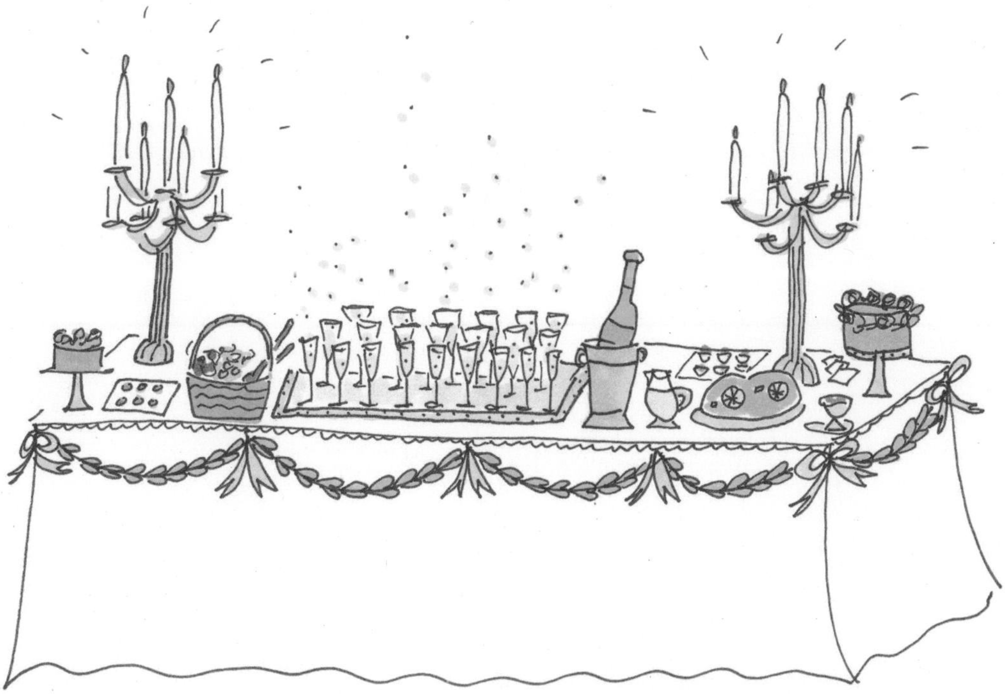

Planning the Wedding

What was important to us?

Easiest and hardest decisions

Funny moments and mishaps

Things we agreed and disagreed upon

Our favorite parts

place photos from the planning stage (tasting, dancing lessons, florist meeting, etc.)

Details of the Day

ceremony location, reception location, invitation, florist, caterer, cake baker, ceremony music, reception music, tent company, lighting company, transportation, rentals, wedding dress, groom's attire, makeup artist, hairstylist, photographer, videographer, wedding planner...

the Wedding Dress

The search: finding THE dress and accessories

dress designed by:

place fabric swatch and photos from fittings

Something Old Something New Something Borrowed Something Blue

Our Wedding Registry

Where we registered

What we wanted most

Our most surprising gifts

Our favorite gifts

attach your bridal registry list

Wedding Guests and Gifts

guest	gift	guest	gift

guest gift guest gift

guest	gift	guest	gift

guest	gift	guest	gift

Bridal Shower

Invitation, theme, menu, who came, what it was like, favorite gifts

place invitation, ribbons, cards, mementos, and photos

The Bachelorette Party

Where it was held, who attended, what HE did that night

place photos and mementos

place photos and mementos

The Bachelor Party

Where it was held, who attended,
what SHE did that night

Our Rehearsal Dinner

Where it was held

Who came

Special presentations

Memorable and outrageous moments

place invitation, toasts, speeches, menu, photos

place wedding invitation here

Our Wedding Invitation

Our R.S.V.P.s

place favorite responses (the first to arrive, most memorable, funniest, most sentimental, etc.)

Guests who traveled the farthest ....

Youngest guest to attend wedding ....

Oldest guest to attend wedding ....

Our Wedding Day

the weather

the President

world events

latest trends

popular songs

popular movies

popular books

popular television shows

Newspaper front page or headlines
from the day of our wedding

Wedding Day Timetable

Bride's day

7:30 am ....

8 am ....

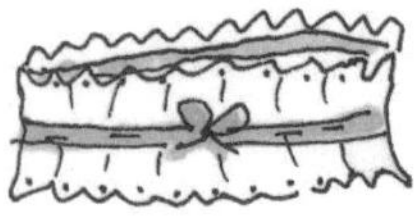

8:30 am ....

9 am ....

9:30 am ....

10 am ....

10:30 am ....

11 am ....

11:30 am ....

12 pm ....

12:30 pm ....

1 pm ....

1:30 pm ....

2 pm ....

2:30 pm ....

3 pm ....

3:30 pm ....

4 pm ....

4:30 pm ....

5 pm ....

5:30 pm ....

6 pm ....

6:30 pm ....

7 pm ....

7:30 pm ....

Groom's day

7:30 am

8 am

8:30 am

9 am

9:30 am

10 am

10:30 am

11 am

11:30 am

12 pm

12:30 pm

1 pm

1:30 pm

2 pm

2:30 pm

3 pm

3:30 pm

4 pm

4:30 pm

5 pm

5:30 pm

6 pm

6:30 pm

7 pm

7:30 pm

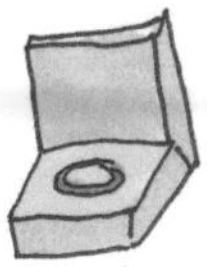

Our Bridal Party

name and role

relationship to bride and groom

place bridal party photos

Our Wedding Ceremony

Where it took place, Officiant, Order of ceremony,
What we were thinking while up there, Favorite moment

place ceremony photo or wedding program here (write your vows, special prayers, rituals, or readings—any personal touches)

Wedding Ceremony

decorations and details

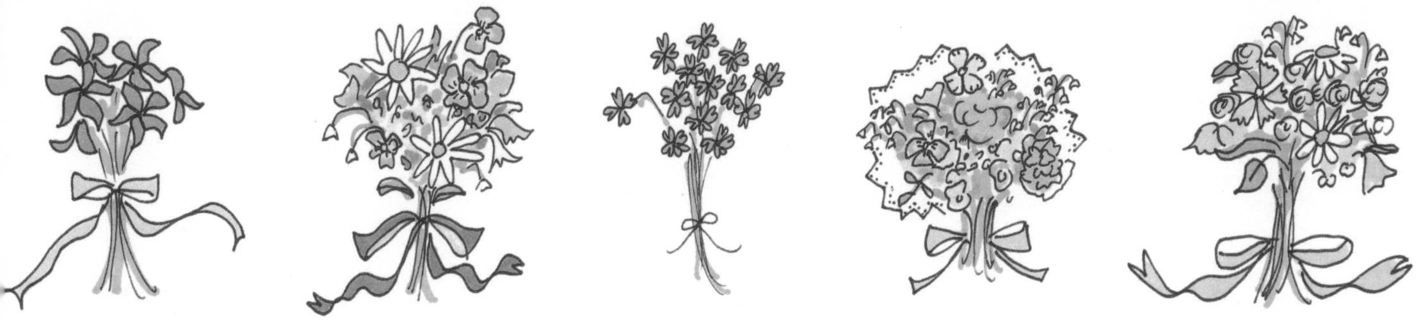

place photo of bouquet or place envelope containing
pressed flower and swatch of ribbon from bouquet

Bride's Bouquet

TO PRESS A FLOWER: *Place a few blooms from your bouquet in between the pages of a book (weight with more books on top) and allow two weeks to dry. Place in envelope here (glassine or transparent would be best!).*

Wedding Reception

Where it took place and what it looked like

describe or place photos or examples of centerpieces and floral decorations, escort cards, place cards, seating chart (reduced size), cocktail napkins, favor, and other details

table 1
GROOM
BRIDE

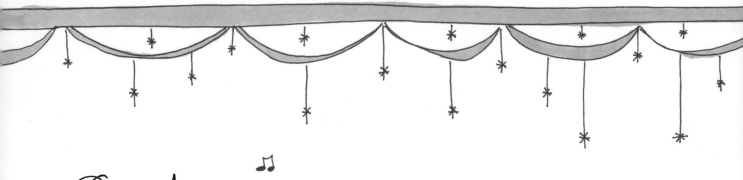

Our Music

for the ceremony

for the reception

special songs

Our song was...

place photos from first dance and other special dances

Our First Dance

Our Menu

place menu card or describe menu

Our Wedding Cake

flavor, frosting, filling, and decoration

place photo of cake or cake cutting

Toasts

place copies of your toasts or write favorite lines here. . . place photo of your favorite toast being given

Cheers!

Favorite Moments from Our Celebration

Our Wedding Memories

What we remember most

What made us laugh

What made us cry

the day after the wedding, write down your thoughts and memories of the most special moments from the rehearsal through the wedding (place in envelope here)

Favorite Wedding Snapshots

Our Wedding Night and the Day After

place photos and mementos: hotel check-in card or copy of your reservation as a married couple, label from champagne bottle, invitation to a post-wedding brunch, etc.

Our Honeymoon

itinerary and favorite moments

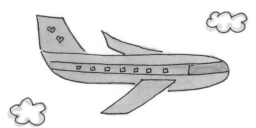

write your initials on the suitcase and place photos

Souvenirs, menus, matchbooks, cards, maps, local currency, ticket stubs

Our Honeymoon

Send yourselves a postcard and place here

Newlyweds

Wedding announcement and notes from friends and family

place wedding announcement from your newspaper, thank you notes, change of address notice

Highlights from Our First Year of Marriage

Where we lived

What we learned about each other

The biggest surprise

Happy Anniversary

traditional gifts by year	our gifts to each other	how we celebrated
1st · paper		
2nd · cotton		
3rd · leather		
4th · linen		
5th · wood		
6th · iron		
7th · wool		
8th · bronze		
9th · pottery		
10th · tin		
11th · steel		
12th · silk		
13th · lace		
14th · ivory		
15th · crystal		
20th · china		
25th · silver		
30th · pearl		
35th · coral		
40th · ruby		
45th · sapphire		
50th · gold		
55th · emerald		
60th · diamond		

...And They Lived Happily Ever After
forever

Printed in China. ISBN 0-06-073521-X